UNDERWATER GUIDE to the FLORIDA KEYS

Text and Photography
by Stephen Frink

Blue Water Publishing, Inc.
Key Largo, Florida

Text and Photos © 1990 Stephen Frink

All rights reserved. No part of this book may be reproduced in any form whatsoever without written permission of the publisher.

ISBN Number 0-9625409-0-0

Published by  Blue Water Publishing, Inc.
Key Largo, Florida

First Printing   March 1990

Acknowledgements: This book is dedicated to the professional dive operators of the Florida Keys. They entered this business out of a love for underwater adventure, and continue to share that affection for the coral reef with their visitors.

For additonal copies, please send 7.95 plus 3.00 handling and postage to:

Blue Water Publishing, Inc.
P.O. Box 2720
Key Largo, FL 33037

Front Cover: Barbara Doernbach views school of bluestriped grunt in elkhorn coral at Pickles Reef.

Inside Front Cover: A dense school of blackbar soldierfish at Ten Fathom Ledge off Key West.

Inside Back Cover: Florida Keys charter dive boat moored above Middle Keys coral reef.

PRINTED IN THE UNITED STATES OF AMERICA

TABLE OF CONTENTS

Introduction	5
History of the Florida Keys	7
The Keys Today	13
Mile Marker System	15
Climate	17
Diving the Florida Keys	21
Reef Etiquette	24
Photo Etiquette	25
Keys Dive Sites	27
Upper Keys	27
Florida Keys Map	32
Middle Keys	45
Lower Keys	49
Key West	51
Conclusion	59
Fish Identification	60

Introduction

I have lived in the Florida Keys for more than a decade. While this may not qualify me as a native "conch", I've been here long enough to observe the inevitable changes and trends. My business is underwater photography, and in the pursuit of underwater images I have had the opportunity to dive extensively throughout the Keys. This book will highlight some of my underwater experiences in both words and photos.

I have also been fortunate enough to be sent on assignment to most of the other diving hot spots throughout the world. My editorial and personal projects have taken me repeatedly to the Cayman Islands, Bonaire, Belize, the British Virgin Islands, the Bahamas, and the Bay Islands of Honduras. I have also gone to the Red Sea, Australia, Truk Lagoon, Belau, the Sea of Cortez, and even the Kenya Coast on photo expeditions. Yet home is the Florida Keys, and this is an area that continually provides tremendous diving enjoyment.

In terms of sheer numbers of visiting divers, the Florida Keys comprise the world's most popular underwater attraction. For those who know where to look, there are historical and modern shipwrecks, drift dives, shallow coral reefs, dropoffs, and an amazing abundance of tropical marine life. This book is intended to celebrate the beauty of the world beneath Keys' seas, and assist our visitors in their quest for the best available underwater experience.

Left: Stephen Frink on location in the Red Sea, photographing a large anemone cluster filled with clownfish and domino damselfish.
© *1990 Barbara Doernbach*

History of the Florida Keys

To the Spaniards they were "Los Martires". Members of Ponce De Leon's 1513 expedition first viewed the tangled, twisted shapes of the islands in the far distance and called them "the martyrs" for the pain and suffering their appearance suggested. It is ironic that this earliest appellation was applied to what has become the world's most popular watersports vacation destination.

Just in the Key Largo National Marine Sanctuary it is estimated that one million divers and snorkelers visit annually. To this huge population, factor in fishermen, families viewing the coral reefs for the first time from a glass bottom boat, and pleasure boaters; and the numbers swell to at least 1.5 million watersports enthusiasts in the Upper Keys alone. Statistics are more difficult to ascertain for the remainder of the Florida Keys, but if only another 500,000 were to visit the Middle Keys, Lower Keys, and Key West (and this is very conservative), there could be 2 million visitors to the coral reefs of the Florida Keys each year. This population of divers is larger than that which visits Hawaii, the Pacific, or even the Caribbean taken as a cumulative whole. Why then is this destination so popular?

Long before the Florida Keys became a watersports mecca, in fact before man, the Keys fought for their terrestrial existence with the sea. Geologists suggest that the Florida Keys may be 100,000 years old, but exact geological data is vague because the coral, limestone, and oolite foundation of the islands has emerged and been submerged into the surrounding seas at least four times since the Pleistocene Era. In ancient times these islands were but patches of coral awash in a tropical southern sea. As the ocean receded most recently, the coral reefs became exposed to the sun and winds. The corals died but left their calcareous exoskeletons to anchor the soil and vegetation that

Left: The marine life of the Florida Keys is rich and abundant both on the coral reefs of the Atlantic Ocean and the nutirient rich shallows of the Florida Bay and Gulf of Mexico. This seahorse was photographed among the turtle grasses located on the bay side off Key Largo.

makes up the over 200 islands and cayes now known as the Florida Keys.

Mangrove trees were probably among the first forms of vegetation, securing and protecting the islands from the ravages of the sea. Later came the palm trees, flowering tropical plants, and lush hardwood hammock that carpets much of the Keys. Over the years the islands have grown and matured so that now they separate the shallow flats of the Florida Bay and Gulf of Mexico to the west from the crystalline waters of the Atlantic Ocean to the east.

As the islands evolved, gradually more coral reefs formed offshore to replace those left high and dry by the sea's recession. Today there exists an extensive fringing reef system four to six miles to seaward, and paralleling the entire length of the Keys. While there may be patches of coral evident in South Florida waters to the north of the Florida Keys, nowhere else in North America features the density, diversity, and beauty of coral reef which so magnificently typifies the underwater resource just seaward of the Florida Keys.

The beauty and bounty of the sea meant as much to the earliest inhabitants of these islands as it does to the ecologically aware dive tourist of today. The fierce Vescaynos and Matecumbeses Indians maintained no permanent villages, but traveled from island to caye in their piroques living on fish, turtles, shellfish, and manatees. The Calusa Indians populated the Keys somewhat later, and to an extent coexisted with the Spaniards who came to the Keys primarily to salvage their treasure galleons which had run aground on the extensive reefline. The Calusas ultimately were victimized by Spanish slavers and decimated by the diseases of the New World, and by the time the Spanish departed the Keys, what few Calusas remained were ultimately displaced by settlers

The mangrove tree serves to anchor and protect the fragile landmass of the Floida Keys.

from the Bahamas.

The last Indian influence in the Florida Keys were by the fierce Seminoles who roamed the Everglades and the Keys with increasingly hostile raiding parties. When Jacob Housman, a former wrecker from Key West who came to develop a settlement on Indian Key, sought a government contract to exterminate Seminoles at $200.00 per head, Chief Chekika took it personally and on August 7, 1840 led his warriors to loot and burn Indian Key. Sixteen of the fifty-five settlers on the island died, and in reprisal U.S. troops under Colonel William Harney virtually eradicated the Seminoles in a confrontation near Lake Okeechobee. This left the Florida Keys free to develop, but since the only significant natural resource available was the sea, the industry and commerce of the Florida keys has always been directly tied to the coral reef.

Indian Key was a flourishing community until destroyed by the Seminole Indians in 1840. (Harpers New Monthly)

The 1733 FLEET – Rodrigo de Torres was one who came to know these reefs with too much intimacy. As the commander of a fleet of ships laden with a consignment of 12.4 million pesos in silver and gold extracted from the New World (plus an incredible amount of contraband treasure, cleverly hidden within the ships' holds to cheat the King from his share of treasure), General de Torres departed Havana harbor under a bad omen on Friday the 13th, 1733 intending a return voyage to Spain. News of tropical storms moved only as fast as the fastest sailing ship, and de Torres had no way of knowing about the immense storm system that was even then devastating the Lesser Antilles and following a destructive sweep north.

By the second day at sea the fleet had sighted the Florida Keys when the wind shifted from the east and increased in velocity. The clouds darkened and the color of the sea changed from deep indigo to ominous gray.

Gusts raged through the rigging and ripped at the canvas while the seas became more confused. The rains came in torrents and the decks were awash with breaking, whitecapped waves. The signal was hoisted to divert the fleet to deeper water, but by then it was too late. The fleet was at the mercy of the relentless storm, but there was no mercy. By nightfall almost all of the ships had been driven westward and scattered, smashed and sunken along eighty miles of Florida Keys reefline.

The Spaniards quickly sent out rescue vessels to pick up the survivors who were by then building crude shelters from the debris and camping out along the shore. The Spaniards were well organized for salvage, and the remains of the fleet were either refloated or burned to the waterline to better enable divers to descend into the cargo holds to extract treasure. This also served to help hide the ship's from freebooters, and while guardships provided security, the salvage work proceeded for several years. When the salvage was finally terminated, the final count revealed even more gold and silver than was on the original manifest, of course due to smuggling.

Hurricanes sank many Spanish galleons throughout the Florida Keys. (Archives of Seville)

For the next 200 years, these remnants of the 1733 fleet went largely undisturbed except by drifting sand and wave action. General Torres' flagship the CAPTINA was the first to be discovered in recent times. Discovered in the 1930s by a Keys fisherman, Tavernier based hard hat diver Art McKee later explored the wreck site and found some silver coins and a gold escudo dated 1721. After more research in the Archive of the Indies in Spain and a decade of underwater exploration, McKee ultimately uncovered the massive ballast pile, ship's timbers, 20 cannons, more than 1,000 silver coins, statues and religious medals, jewelry, and ship's weapons. By 1949 McKee had amassed a huge inventory of historically significant artifacts, and he opened a museum in Tavernier to display his treasures. He operated a glass-bottom boat to share the wrecksites with tourists, and even let them dive with hard hat gear occasionally. McKee also opened the door for scores of other treasure divers who worked the shallow reefs of the Florida Keys in search of further remains of the 1733 fleet.

From the mid-1950s through the late 1960s several treasure salvors worked the wrecks of the 1733 fleet with varying degrees of success. Ships including the TRES PUENTES, EL INFANTE, ALMIRANTA, CHAVES, HERRERA, LERRI, SAN PEDRO, EL SUECO DE ARIZON, POPULO, ANGUSTIAS, and SAN JOSE have since been discovered, with the trend of discovery suggesting that the heavier galleons struck the offshore reef and dropped their treasure and artifacts on the inside reef. The smaller ships probably rode over the fringing reef on storm driven swells, only to be sucked towards the channels separating the Keys and run aground in shallow water. Private salvors extracted much of the treasure, although archaeological priorities were minimal during those early years of exploration. Many of these wrecksites will still yield an occasional artifact or coin to careful scrutiny and hand fanning. More importantly, they represent a sort of underwater museum, a portal to the rich marine heritage of the Florida Keys.

Presently there are plans being developed to establish an underwater archaeological preserve in the Florida Keys to both educate visitors and enhance access to these sites. The first developed site is the underwater remains of the SAN PEDRO, situated off Indian Key in just 18 feet of water. The 287 ton Dutch-built vessel was carrying 16,000 pesos of silver and numerous crates of Chinese porcelain, Mexican ceramics, and animal skins. Since the 1733

Treasure salvor Carl Fismer has explored many of the shipwrecks of the 1733 fleet, and has discovered coins and fascinating artifacts among the wreckage.

Moray eels are typical inhabitants of the historical shipwrecks throughout the Florida Keys.

hurricane drove the ship aground most of the "treasure" has been reclaimed, but there still exists the ballast pile (composed of river rock and cut quarry rock), wooden hull remants, and abundant marine life. Several species of coral have anchored to the debris and pufferfish, barracuda, angelfish, moray eels, and grunts now reside. In addition seven replica cannons were cast in concrete from a mold based on a gun from the SAN JOSE, and these have been placed around the wreck to lend a further sense of authenticity. Located in Hawk Channel, the visibility on the SAN PEDRO is often fair, but the waters this near shore will never be a translucent as the reefs farther offshore which are washed by the cleansing currents of the Gulf Stream.

The Keys Today

One of the most significant factors in developing the Florida Keys in modern times was the construction of Henry Flagler's "Railroad That Went To Sea", ultimately in a literal sense. Prior to the construction of the railroad linking Key West with mainland Florida, inter-island transportation could only be accomplished by boat, a slow, expensive, and relatively inefficient process. When the Key West extension of the Florida East Coast Railway was complete, 29 emerald-hued islands were connected via sturdy bridges and embankments. Tourists could travel in style and comfort down the 106 mile stretch of the Florida Keys from Key Largo to the north all the way to Key West at the southernmost tip. At Key West, ships would then transport gamblers and sun worshippers to the casinos and beaches of Cuba.

The Overseas Railroad, alternately called "Flagler's Folly" and the "Eighth Wonder of the World", defied the winds and weather of the Atlantic Ocean for 23 years until a tragic hurricane September 2, 1935 brought an end to the venture. It took 12 years and $27 million pre-depression dollars to connect the Florida Keys, but just a few hours of 200 mile an hour hurricane-driven winds and waves brought the demise of Flagler's dream.

During the Depression the Overseas Railroad went into receivership, and the railroad right-of-way and still standing bridges were sold to the government for $640,000. Given the cost of waterfront property in the Keys today, this proved one of Florida's best real estate bargains, and allowed U.S. #1, the concrete auto artery so essential to Key's commerce, to be superimposed over the railway's former path. By March 28, 1938 the Overseas Highway was open to traffic. The era of the automobile had come to the Florida Keys and the legend "The Islands You Can Drive To" became reality.

The Overseas Highway connecting the Florida Keys is one of America's most interesting and scenic highways.

The Florida Keys are accessible by boat or by airplane, with dozens of marinas throughout the islands and airstrips at the Ocean Reef Club in North Key Largo (private) and in Marathon and Key West (public). However, automobiles carry by far the greatest number of visitors to the Keys. The Overseas Highway has been significantly improved since the days when Franklin Roosevelt was the first American president to be driven from Miami to Key West. Even in my recent memory the Keys have been made safer and easier to travel.

I remember my first trip across the narrow, two lane Seven Mile Bridge. To call it unsettling was an understatement. There were no shoulders on the bridge, and when a car broke down, traffic simply stopped. The road was so narrow that when two trucks passed in opposite directions their mirrors would sometimes collide, and when a huge 18 wheeler barreled down the road at 70 MPH, the buffeting of the truck's passing wake made the azure depths of the seas below seem all too near. The new Seven Mile Bridge is a tremendous improvement. Now four lanes wide with broad shoulders on either side, the Seven Mile Bridge (along with the other safe and modern bridges in place elsewhere in the Keys), makes the trip much more enjoyable. With the deep blue of the Atlantic Ocean to the left of the southbound motorist, and the rich emerald hues of the Florida Bay and Gulf of Mexico to the right, the Overseas Highway traversing the Florida Keys is one of America's most fascinating road journeys.

The new Seven Mile Bridge is one of the many recent improvements to the Overseas Highway.

Mile Marker System

Of the over 200 islands comprising the Keys archipelago, 30 are now linked by the bridges and roadways of U.S. #1. In fact, U.S. #1 is so integral to the commerce of the Keys that locations are generally referred to according to "Mile Marker" position. While U.S. #1 actually runs the length of the eastern seaboard from Maine to Key West, Mile Marker references in the Keys originate at #0 at the Monroe County courthouse in Key West and pass through the Monroe County line at about Mile Marker 112 north of Key Largo.

The major centers of population will be clustered as follows:

Key West - MM0 through MM18
Lower Keys - MM19 - MM45
Middle Keys - MM46 - MM60
Upper Keys - MM61 - MM106

Small green informational signs will designate each mile marker and provide a directional heading. If the numbers decrease you are headed south towards Key West, if they increase, you are on a northerly route towards Key Largo.

The green mile marker numbers along the shoulder of the Overseas Highway refer to the distance north of the Monroe County Courthouse in Key West (Mile Marker 0).

Climate

The Florida Keys are located in the confluence of the temperate and tropic zones. The Tropic of Cancer which officially separates temperate from tropic lies 70 miles south of Key West, but the tropical influence is strong throughout the Keys. The northward flow of the Gulf Stream, a huge offshore current bringing warm, clear, and low nutrient waters past the Florida Keys, also brings warmth to the islands. This, combined with the prevailing tropical tradewinds, helps to make the Keys balmy the year round.

Unlike our northern neighbors with four distinct seasons, Keys' primary seasonal distinctions are summer and winter. For general tourism, winter is considered "high" season and hotels operate at their highest average occupancy. The mean air temperature is 74 degrees, and a daytime high of 80 degrees is not unusual. In the evening it may drop into the 60s, so sweaters are advisable occasionally. During the winter several cold fronts should be expected to descend from the north. Local residents will dig out their jackets, but visitors acclimated to northern winters will get sunburned from lying around the pool. During these northers the winds will increase in intensity, and generally make sea conditions rough and underwater visibility inevitably diminished.

Divers visiting the Keys during the winter months can expect an occasional day of exceptional visibility in the 100 foot range, but average sea conditions will be more like 30 to 50 feet of lateral visibility. The best visibility I have ever encountered in the Keys was on a day in late November diving the wreck of the U.S. Coast Guard cutter DUANE. The ship is 327 feet long and I could see at least 2/3rds of her length in a single glance. This was true 200 foot visibility, and in areas washed by the Gulf Stream, this can happen with some regularity. On rare occasions the clarity may drop below

Left: The sunset over the Florida Bay off Key Largo provides a spectacular backdrop for angling efforts.

30 feet in conjunction with a heavy wind condition, but when the winds shift or abate, the seas can clear up with a single tidal cycle.

Note also that heavy winds alone do not necessarily mean bad diving conditions. An onshore wind may help to push the magnificent clarity of the Gulf Stream closer to the reefline. Although Keys' dive sites are generally to the windward side of the islands, occasionally the wind can shift enough to leave the reef in a temporary lee of the land mass. In determining how the wind will affect dive options, both direction and intensity of wind must be considered.

Since the Keys curve in a long arc to the West, the same prevailing wind will not necessarily affect all of the Keys identically. It could be rough in Key Largo and calm in Key West, or vice versa. Further, the weather forecast broadcast by Miami radio and television stations bears only a passing similarity to the conditions prevalent in the Keys on any given day since the larger land mass of the Florida mainland attracts more inclement weather than occurs in the Keys.

The Florida Keys dive operator will generally be able to give an accurate appraisal of the dive conditions, particularly if the inquiry is made after 10:00 A.M.. By then the morning dive trips will have had a chance to arrive at the reef and report. Most will truthfully report conditions, but also be aware that these folks are in business to carry divers to the reefs. Their business is ill-served by exaggerating the severity of weather conditions. Weather reports may be further confirmed by listening to local Keys radio stations which often include fishing and diving reports. NOAA weather forecasts are broadcast on VHF radios and on the local Keys television station. The dockmaster at most marinas will be happy to pass on weather information as well.

The U.S. Coast Guard Cutter DUANE was intentionally sunk as a dive attraction just south of the Key Largo National Marine Sanctuary, and now sits upright in 120 feet of water.

The water temperature in the winter may drop to 68 degrees (which is also the lower limit at which corals can survive), but most of the time 72 to 76 degrees is a more reasonable expectation. The closer the dive site is to the influence of the Gulf Stream, the warmer the site will be. Most of the time I am most comfortable diving the Keys in winter wearing a 3/16 inch wetsuit for thermal protection, but then I think your blood "thins" a bit after a few years of living in the tropics. Most of our warmer-blooded visitors find that a 1/8 inch wetsuit or even a dive skin is adequate. Still, for the hour-long dives that are possible due to the shallow depths of most Keys sites, the thermal protection of a wetsuit is certainly advisable in winter.

Summer may be the "low" season in terms of hotel rates, but it is the prime season in terms of dive adventure. The water temperature will rise to the mid-80s, wetsuits are no longer necessary, and the days of 100 foot visibility become much more common (although 50 to 80 feet is more the norm). The seas are usually calm, and this combination of great conditions, better hotel rates, and vacation synchronicity make June, July, and August the most popular months in terms of the number of visiting divers. Savvy divers also realize that September and October feature these same superior conditions, but with less crowded dive boats and bargain hotel rates.

The moon jellyfish is commonly sighted in shallow water along the coral reef throughout the Keys.

Diving The Florida Keys

GENERAL OBSERVATIONS - As a diver visiting the Florida Keys, your first and most important insight should be that THERE IS NO BEACH DIVING IN THE FLORIDA KEYS! I say this with emphasis because I am also involved in the retail dive business and have repeatedly heard our visitors ask where they can go diving from the shore. This is not to say that shore diving is restricted or illegal, but to confirm that it simply will not be good. Without question, the best diving in the Florida Keys occurs around the coral reefs, and these are located four to six miles offshore.

Near shore the seas will be generally turbid and the bottom characterized by a sand and mud punctuated by turtle grass and an occasional coral outcropping. At about three to four miles offshore there tends to be more scattered coral heads, and the water clarity is better on average. The true fringing coral reef people travel to the Keys to experience is usually found at least five miles to seaward and runs parallel to the islands. A spur and groove coral formation perpendicular to the shoreline provides the protection and sustenance necessary to nourish the incredibly rich marine life found in the Florida Keys. While a snorkel trip through the mangrove canals lining the coast can provide a fascinating glimpse of a remarkable ecosystem, seeing the best of Keys underwater beauty requires boat transportation.

Boat transportation to the reefs can be by private pleasure craft, rental boat, or via a commercial dive operation, of which there are scores up and down the 106 mile chain of islands. For those who would like to dive from a commercial boat (or even have their scuba cylinders refilled), be aware that a scuba certification card will be required. It is also a good idea to bring a logbook as an indicator of experience level when visiting the Keys. Given

Left: The very best diving in the Florida Keys is five to six miles offshore, and features clear tropical water and abundant marine life.

the number of divers who visit each year, some will certainly be experienced, but many others will be novices, perhaps experiencing their first warm water dive adventures. In order to provide a safe underwater experience and structure the dives to the needs and abilities of their guests, Keys dive operators are turning ever more towards logbook inspection as a gauge of experience level.

For dive operators, carrying passengers aboard "boats for hire" comes under the regulation of the U.S. Coast Guard. The commercial dive boats will therefore have been Coast Guard inspected and deemed seaworthy, and the captains shall have passed the required boating competency tests. This Coast Guard monitoring and the level of competition between dive shops helps to keep the charter fleet in top shape. The most impressive vessels will be 25 to 65 feet long, accommodate 6 to 48 passengers, and be customized for diver convenience with a walk-through transom and dive platform with extended ladders, tank racks, camera rinse, VHF radio, protection from sea spray and sun, and carry diver safety items such as oxygen and first aid supplies. The Keys Association of Dive Operators has determined a code of ethics for the services and professionalism among its members, and this has become the standard for dive operations throughout the Keys.

The dive charter boats of the Florida Keys are Coast Guard certified and may accommodate from 6 to 48 passengers.

The dives on most of the coral reefs throughout the Keys are relatively shallow (20 to 45 feet), and most often are NOT conducted as guided dives. There will be a captain and mate on the boat ready to assist should a diving problem occur, but the diver's buddy is considered the most direct form of aid in an emergency. Divers are assumed to be responsible and able to tour the reef at their own pace. They are generally expected to be back on board the dive boat with 500 psi remaining in their tanks. Should a guided dive be desired in order to refresh rusty diving skills, or simply to assure that the best portions of the reef will be viewed, it should be arranged before the dive boat leaves the dock.

Scuba instruction at all levels from open water through instructor certification is available, and specialties such as underwater photography are especially well served. Quick E-6 film processing is available in Key Largo, Islamorada, Marathon, and Key West; and one hour print processing is available in virtually all centers of population.

Instruction in underwater still and video may be booked, and still and video cameras are available for rent or sale at several locations. In the Florida Keys you can rent dive scooters, train to be an aquanaut, or even book into a plush hotel to spend the night beneath the surface of a mangrove lagoon. If it has to do with diving or some level of diving service, it is likely available somewhere in the Florida Keys.

Underwater video and still photography are popular activities among Keys' dive enthusiasts.

Reef Etiquette

The National Marine Sanctuaries have published a reef etiquette guide to aid in the enjoyment of their beautiful resources. The following paraphrased guidelines will assist compliance with regulations throughout the Keys:

• Just touching coral causes damage to the fragile polyps. Therefore do not allow hands, knees, tank or fins to contact the coral at any time.

• Do not allow your anchor, anchor line or chain to contact the corals. Many areas are moving towards the use of mooring buoys to help reduce the risk of anchor damage, and these should always be used when available.

• Spearfishing in Looe Key, Pennekamp Park, or the Key Largo National Marine Sanctuaries is not permitted. Hook and line fishing is allowed but applicable size, catch limits, and seasons must be observed.

• Hand feeding of fish is discouraged because of the risk of injury to the diver, possibility of introducing disease to the fish, and because it changes the natural behavior of the fish.

• Spiny lobster size and season restrictions must be observed, and in the core area of the Looe Key National Marine Sanctuary it is prohibited altogether. This prohibition is because it is virtually impossible to catch lobster without touching, and thereby damaging, the corals.

• Corals, shells, starfish and other animals can not be removed within a Sanctuary, and coral collection is absolutely prohibited throughout the Keys.

• Regulations prohibit littering or discharge of any substance except chum.

• Fines are imposed within the Sanctuaries for running aground or otherwise damaging the corals.

• Historical artifacts within the Sanctuaries are protected by federal law, and those found within the three mile limit are protected by state statutes.

• The red and white diver down flag or international alpha flag must be displayed while diving or snorkeling. Boats must go slow enough so as to leave no wake within 100 yards of a dive flag.

Photo Etiquette

To this list I'd like to add a few personal observations pertinent to underwater photographers:

• If a photographer is in the process of photographing a particular subject that you would also like to photograph, settle gently to the sand out of camera range and wait patiently. Do not approach until the other photographer abandons the subject.

• Be careful of fin activity in the vicinity of an underwater photographer. Being overweighted and kicking off the bottom can render an area unsuitable for photography very quickly due to particulate matter suspended in the water.

• If you see a camera (or several cameras) situated carefully on the bottom, the chances are it is not lost. The photographer it belongs to is quite likely nearby and is taking pictures with yet another camera system. That photographer will be distressed to see you swimming off with what you assume to be a newly acquired prize.

Keys Dive Sites

Each of the geographic areas of the Florida Keys has a slightly different flavor, both above and below the surface, and each tends to attract its own loyal following. To help visitors decide which area is best for their vacation, the following is an overview of Keys' dive attractions taken in order of geographic placement, from north to south:

Upper Keys

Key Largo, Tavernier, and Islamorada comprise the primary centers of population in the Upper Keys. North of Key Largo there is the Ocean Reef Club, an exclusive residential community with its own professional diving services and marina, but Ocean Reef is generally inaccessible to the average tourist. Key Largo is the site of the John Pennekamp Coral Reef State Park and the adjacent Key Largo National Marine Sanctuary. There is some ongoing confusion between the nomenclature in terms of where the best diving occurs, even though many dive shops use the name "Pennekamp" interchangeably with the Key Largo National Marine Sanctuary.

As clarification, remember that the Keys feature fringing reefs four to six miles offshore. The shoreline is tremendously important in terms of maintaining the quality of the water on the reef, and to that end the John Pennekamp Coral Reef State Park protects the shoreline within its boundaries, as well as the shallow waters to about three miles offshore. It is this attraction, with an entrance located at Mile Marker 103, that the State of Florida maintains with campgrounds, beaches, boat ramps, and a visitor center with an aquarium. The Park attracts more than 500,000 visitors annually through its gates, and the Pennekamp concessionaire on the Park grounds provides dive and snorkel boat charters, glass bottom boats, and rental sailboats and canoes.

The Key Largo National Marine Sanctuary

Left: The deep water gorgonia pictured here has grown on the crow's nest of the USCGC BIBB in just one year, and as the shipwreck matures, even more coral and marine life will accumulate.

The mangrove lined seashore in the Florida Keys provides habitat for both marine life and birds.

Divers to the Florida Keys should be especially careful with anchor placement and buoyancy control. The corals are fragile and repeated contact can kill the polyps, as is seen here in the contrast between a living coral head on the right, and the damaged, dead coral colony.

boundary abuts that of Pennekamp at sea, and runs from the three mile limit to the 300 foot depth contour. Management of the Key Largo National Marine Sanctuary is federal and Pennekamp Park is under State of Florida jurisdiction. The combined Park and Sanctuary encompasses a total area of 183 square miles, but it is within Sanctuary waters that virtually all of the best diving occurs. Whatever the semantics, Pennekamp Park and the Key Largo National Marine Sanctuary comprise one of America's most precious natural assets.

In the early days of Florida tourism a sea life novelty trade was sytematically stripping the Keys of its coral and shells. More tourists were visiting, even in the late 1930s, and coral was being harvested with the aid of crowbars and small seagoing cranes. Commercial shell collectors were further decimating the reef in search of specimens. The whole scene was fortunately appalling to those with vision, and in 1957 a biological conference held in the Everglades National Park included a stirring presentation by Dr. Gilbert Voss of the Marine Institute of the University of Miami whereby he outlined the desecration of the reefs. The National Audubon Society, University of Florida, and Miami Herald, under the direction of editor John Pennekamp supported a proposal for protection of the area by creating the first underwater park.

On December 3, 1959 the control of the ocean bottom to the three mile limit was transferred to the Florida Board of Parks and Historic Memorials, and on March 15, 1960 President Eisenhower placed the remaining areas beyond the three mile limit and to the edge of the Continental Shelf under the control of the Secretary of the Interior as a permanent preserve. The marine life and corals off Key Largo now had protection.

The popularity of scuba diving within the Sanctuary is apparent with the proliferation of dive services evident along U.S. #1 and the deep water canals leading to the Atlantic. The red and white divers down flag is a familiar complement to the Key Largo skyline, and each of these shops will feature daily trips to the reefs of the Sanctuary. Since the protected area includes a 25 mile stretch of reefline, in addition to being 6 miles offshore, it is clear that no single dive operator will dive all of the Key Largo National Marine Sanctuary. It is just too large an area. Nor will you see it all in the course of a week's dive vacation. I know I have yet to see it all, and I've been diving here for more than twelve years. Some of the more popular sites are as follows:

CARYSFORT REEF is situated near the northern boundary of the Key Largo National Marine Sanctuary and is obviously marked by a 112 foot lighted steel tower, the first of the navigational lighthouses erected in the Florida Keys. Named originally for the HMS CARYSFORD run aground here in 1770, the reef today exhibits an unusual configuration of hard corals in the shallows which gradually thin out as the depth increases. Fire corals, elkhorn, and staghorn corals intermingle with brain and star coral in the shallows, and as the reef slopes to seaward a limestone bottom decorated with soft corals and gorgonia predominates. This limestone and sand bottom extends to a depth of about 65 feet, at which point a channel of fine sand about 100 feet wide separates the primary reef from a second offshore reef which rises again to a depth of 35 feet before once again sloping off to seaward.

This "double reef" is a geologic anomaly (by Keys standards), and provides refuge for a wide variety of reef tropicals. Schooling grunts will be found in abundance, and an assortment

An aerial view of Carysfort Reef shows the ample coral concentrations in shallow water.

of angelfish, butterflyfish, parrotfish, pufferfish, and other reef dwellers will be commonly sighted.

Since the reef is washed by the Gulfstream, both clear waters and pelagic encounters are the norm. One of the real advantages to Carysfort is that not many boats will typically visit this reef, not because it is not good diving (it is), but because it is a longer boat ride than most. It is the nearest dive site for the dive boats from Ocean Reef, but from Key Largo there are several closer dive sites, and Carysfort may be visited only on occasion. Even on one of those magnificent slick calm weekends of the summer, there may be a dozen boats on the Elbow but only three or four on Carysfort, and during the week you might even have the entire reef to yourself for at least part of the day.

The shallow elkhorn gardens of the Florida Keys are accessible to both divers and snorkelers.

SOUTH CARYSFORT has become a new favorite for both divers and snorkelers, owing primarily to the beautiful elkhorn coral gardens spreading as far as the eye can see. The reef is marked by four foot diamond shaped day beacons, and has been accessorized with mooring buoys (as have many of the best dive sites in the Key Largo National Marine Sanctuary). For snorkelers, South Carysfort is a natural favorite.

THE ELBOW is a descriptive term for a reef structure in the northern quadrant of the Sanctuary that juts out like a crooked arm into the blue water of the Gulfstream. In the days preceding adequate navigational charts, the Elbow must have been more than an occasional surprise to mariners plying the Florida Keys, given the number of wrecks now strewn across her coral backbone. The reefs are shallow, and basically spur and groove formations running perpendicular to the shoreline.

Within the Elbow are located some excellent dive sites including the City of Washington shipwreck, Mike's Wreck, South Ledge Drop-off, and the Fingers. The corals are rich and healthy, the visibility generally quite good, but the most unusual aspect of the Elbow is probably the "tame" marine life that has congregated in the area.

When describing any marine life, the phrase "tame" more likely means "desensitized." Fish generally have a healthy fear of divers, and may be difficult to closely approach. In areas like the Pennekamp Park where the fish have been protected from spearfishing since 1960, part of the natural apprehension is displaced by the constant proximity of the divers. When divers further feed the marine life, the natural order of things is additionally offset by classical conditioning, and this is the case on the Elbow.

A tradition of fish feeding on the Elbow has evolved, and the excitement of fish feeding one of the most requested activities among divers visiting the Elbow. Divemasters will often bring dozens of ballyhoo to the reef to feed the barracuda and moray eels, enticing these dangerous predators to dart within inches of the diver to grab the proffered morsels. A few of the more daring ringmasters of this underwater circus may even clench the ballyhoo bill between their teeth while a swift barracuda rushes past to grab the bait. This makes an awesome sight, and even more dramatic photograph, but there are some fish feeding cautions and concerns:

• It is illegal to feed the marine life anything other than "natural" food. This means that ballyhoo or squid may be appropriate, but canned cheese, hot dogs, or sausage is specifically prohibited by Sanctuary regulation. Anything not in their natural diet could introduce disease.

• Since fish feeding disrupts the natural fear in the animal, these fish may be more

Barracuda are frequently encountered on dive sites along the Elbow in the Key Largo National Marine Sanctuary.

FLORIDA KEYS DIVE SITES

1. Carysfort Reef
2. South Carysfort
3. Elbow
4. North North Key Largo Dry Rocks
5. North Key Largo Dry Rocks
6. Key Largo Dry Rocks Christ of the Abyss
7. Grecian Rocks
8. Benwood
9. French Reef
10. White Bank Dry Rocks
11. Molasses Reef
12. USCGC Bibb
13. USCGC Duane
14. Pickles Reef
15. Conch Reef
16. Hens and Chickens Reef
17. Davis Reef
18. Crocker Reef
19. Eagle
20. Alligator Reef
21. Duck Key Wreck
22. Coffins Patch
23. Thunderbolt
24. Delta Shoals
25. Sombrero Reef
26. Seven Mile Bridge Span
27. Looe Key
28. American Shoals
29. Eastern Sambo
30. Middle Sambo
31. Western Sambo
32. Cayman Salvager
33. Eastern Dry Rocks
34. Rock Key
35. Ten Fathom Ledge
36. Sand Key
37. Western Dry Rocks
38. Alexander
39. Curb
40. Wilkes-Barre

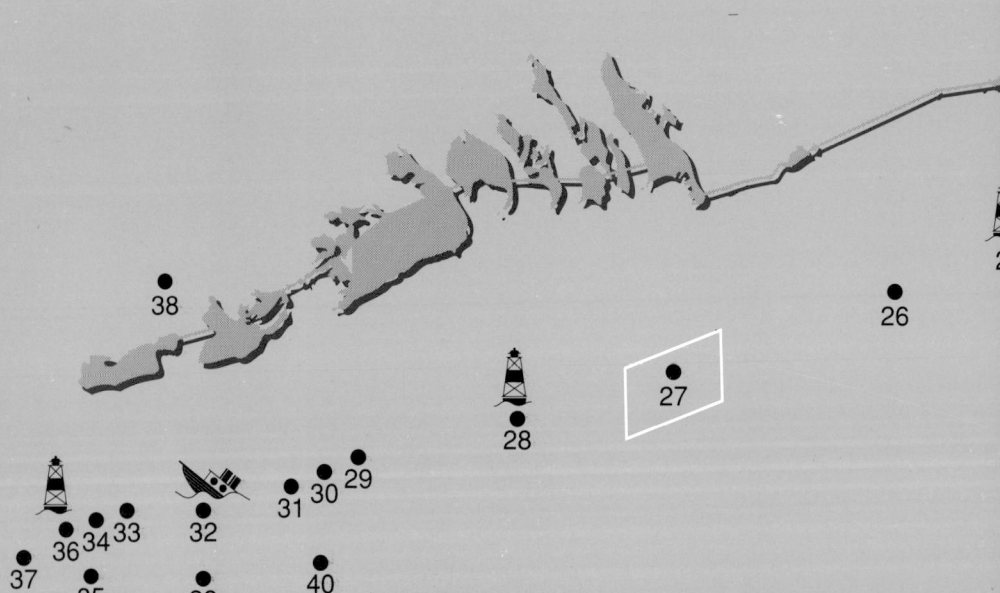

susceptible to hook and line anglers.

• Divers who are not aware that fish on these reefs have been hand fed may find it disconcerting to see a four foot barracuda looming inches from their face mask. The fish is there looking for a handout, and will generally pose no threat to a diver. However, a diver who wiggles their fingers or gestures wildly underwater may appear to the barracuda or eel to be offering bait.

There are usually yellowtail snapper or some other fish around during these fish feeding sessions, and the target species (usually barracuda or eel) have to compete for the bait. They are used to moving quickly, and for the diver whose finger is mistaken for ballyhoo, the result can be disastrous. It is small comfort to realize after the accident that the fish merely made a mistake.

The analogy is the bears in Yellowstone Park. Tourists are not allowed to feed the bears, and Sanctuary rangers may at some point enforce the same feeding restrictions within the waters of the Key Largo and Looe Key National Marine Sanctuaries. Rarely do problems occur, and as an underwater photographer I appreciate the opportunity that fish feeding assures to get close to these normally elusive creatures. I hope we do not require rules to enforce caution among our divers.

The **CITY OF WASHINGTON** represents the remains of a coastal steamer run aground and ultimately dynamited because of its hazard to navigation. Many of the historical shipwrecks in the Keys crashed on shallow reefs with superstructure actually above the waterline. Since other ships could easily smash into the wreckage, these wrecks were sytematically blown apart. The skeletal remnants still have an uncanny ability to attract marine life, and the CITY OF WASHINGTON now hosts a pair of large green moray eels known as Melba and

Scrawled filefish will gently nibble ballyhoo from a diver's hand at Molasses Reef.

Perry, as well as barracuda frequently in residence, and annoyingly aggressive rock hind and yellowtail. When the ballyhoo is out and all the predators are competing for the bait, it is an especially stimulating dive adventure.

In the near vicinity of the CITY OF WASHINGTON is a small wreck featuring ancient timbers still held together by a filigree framework of steel pins known as the **CIVIL WAR WRECK.** This is unmarked by buoys and is inappropriate for more than two or three divers at a time because of its small size. As a result commercial dive boats will rarely visit, which is just as well given the fragility and historical significance of the wreck. Yet the CIVIL WAR WRECK is rich with marine life including at least four spotted moray eels we have come to name Barbara, Slime, Sara, and Leah; as well as large schools of grunt and goatfish, parrotfish, angelfish, and swarms of copper sweeper within the recesses of the hull. Marine archaeologists are still trying to determine with accuracy the age of the wreck, and why it has come to lie in such fascinating decay in 25 feet of water just off the Elbow.

The statue of **CHRIST OF THE ABYSS** has come to be regarded as the symbol of the Sanctuary, having been donated to the Underwater Society of America by dive equipment manufacturer Edigio Cressi and placed beneath the sea on a concrete pedestal in 25 feet of water on the east side of a reef structure known as Dry Rocks. The nine foot tall bronze sculpture is a replica of a statue standing in 50 feet of water off Genoa, Italy. With its arms outstretched, the Keys' version of the Christ figure seems to be beckoning both fish and divers to this lovely inner reef. Given the religious symbolism of the statue, this site is popular for underwater weddings, and at least two dozen of these unique ceremonies have already been performed here.

A spotted moray (top photo) and a green moray eel (bottom photo) are both residents of the CITY OF WASHINGTON shipwreck, located just to the north of the Elbow tower.

The coral reef surrounding the Christ statue is interesting, and well populated with tropical marine life. Smokey, the resident barracuda, is likely one of the world's most frequently photographed fish. Occasionally a green moray known as Sundance will appear, and as on other fish feeding sites, when the bait is extended, there will likely be multiple takers (with yellowtail snapper being the most troublesome). There is one of the Upper Keys largest brain corals situated directly north of the statue, and considering the number of divers who visit this reef annually, I am constantly amazed at the pristine condition of this impressive coral head. Hopefully divers will continue to keep their fins and bodies away from this fragile coral colony, and with the use of the mooring buoys already in place, anchors and chains will not mar its magnificence.

Glass minnows come to the Keys every summer. I'm sure an ichthyologist could explain why they appear when they do and where they come from, but to me its one of the beautiful mysteries of the sea that each year in the same reef areas iridescent silversides swarm. In the Key Largo area, the Minnow Caves at North Dry Rocks, the Benwood Wreck, Hourglass Cave at French Reef, Horseshoe Reef, and the wreck of the Duane are all thick with minnows in mid-summer, and the predators such as grouper, jack, and blue runner are continuously in residence until the schools are depleted.

The **BENWOOD** was one of the hard luck stories of the Florida Coast during World War II. First she was rammed by an American freighter, and then torpedoed by a German U-Boat, and finally she was intentionally run aground to keep from sinking in deep water. This happened in April of 1942, about which time German submarine warfare reached its peak off the Florida coast. In May of 1942 the

Glass minnows are found in huge quanities at many Keys' reef locations, especially in the summer.

Right: The statue of Christ of the Abyss has become the symbol of the Key Largo National Marine Sanctuary and Pennekamp Park.

Navy reported 49 ships torpedoed or shelled, but the Benwood's proximity to the Key Largo coral reef made her more than just a World War II statistic. For many years she sat with her superstructure above the waves, and was the target of military target practice during the 1950s. Pioneer underwater photographer Jerry Greenberg reminisces about the times he would camp out overnight on the deck of the BENWOOD while compiling his early portfolio of the world beneath Keys' seas.

Regrettably, the BENWOOD was one more victim of dynamite in the name of navigational safety, and her superstructure was blown apart.

Still remaining are the deck plating, bow section, ship's ribs, and scattered wreckage lying in water ranging from 25 to 45 feet deep. Copper sweepers inhabit the recesses of the holds, and huge schools of goatfish, grunt, and porkfish cruise the perimeter of the wreck. For macro photographers, the outer hull is a bonanza of Christmas tree worms and other invertebrate life.

The BENWOOD, the Christ of the Abyss statue, and other Sanctuary favorites such as North North Dry Rocks and Minnow Caves, are situated along an inner reef tract. This means that on any given day the water clarity will be less than that found on an outer reef like the Elbow or Molasses Reef. However, when the wind and tides conspire to bring the blue water of the Gulfstream nearer shore, these can be especially captivating dives.

The primary focus of the dive activity on **FRENCH REEF** is the swim-through caves and overhanging ledges that are so prevalent. With openings three to four feet tall carved out of limestone rock by wave action, these caves often lead to large caverns populated by copper sweepers, grouper, and in the summer, glass minnows. The entrance and exit will always be

A school of resident porkfish can be consistently sighted along the bow section of the BENWOOD.

visible, so these caverns do not bear the mystery or danger of deep penetration caves, but at the same time are very beautiful. Mooring buoys mark the finest of the dive sites and permit the boater to easily tie up without risking damage to the precious corals below.

MOLASSES REEF marks the southern boundary of the Sanctuary and is likely the most dived reef in the world. Easily located because its shallows are marked with a 45 foot lighted steel tower, the best diving occurs along the extensive spur and groove coral formations found perpendicular to shore seaward of the tower. Here beautiful high profile corals provide a background for massive schools of grunt and snapper, friendly scrawled filefish, moray eels, Atlantic spadefish, schooling barracuda, snook, inquisitive angelfish, and even an especially approachable southern stingray.

Pelagic life is also common to Molasses. Horse eye jacks, eagle rays, and even hammerhead sharks may possibly enliven the dive, and I've even seen mating hawksbill turtles among the mooring buoys, oblivious to the boating and diver activity all about them.

Molasses Reef is a popular cruising area for Key Largo's glassbottom boats, and recently a 40 foot whale shark swam by one of the boats as if putting on a show for the tourists peering through the viewing windows. In fact, one year while I was in Belize leading a futile whale shark expedition, a whale shark cruised all along the reefline from Molasses to the Elbow. Hundreds of divers got to witness the same sight in my hometown waters that I was half way across the Caribbean pursuing.

Occasionally I do get lucky with the Keys pelagic life however. In two separate, but very special encounters, I was notified by the Key Largo National Marine Sanctuary personnel that something unusual was happening

Glassy sweepers inhabit many of the swim-through caves honeycombing French Reef off Key Largo.

An aerial view of Molasses Reef shows the spur and groove reef structure and the mooring buoys in use to reduce anchor damage.

A mola mola (ocean sunfish) is a rare visitor to Keys' waters.

This immense tiger shark was encountered in 400 feet of water off Key Largo, feeding on a whale carcass.

offshore and was invited to photo document the events. In one case a huge Mola Mola (ocean sunfish) had cruised in behind the reefline at Dry Rocks. This was a fish so massive that in fifteen feet of water its ventral fin scraped the bottom while its dorsal fin broke the surface. These fish are generally encountered only in deep water, and are usually very difficult to approach. Whatever drove the Mola Mola to shallow depths was opportune from a photo perspective.

Another time we received a report from a fishing boat that a whale carcass was floating out in the Gulf Stream attended by a blood slick and half a dozen hungry tiger sharks. This too sounded like a unique photo opportunity, and so we projected the northern flow of the Gulfstream in the time since the first report and launched a search. Luckily we found (or perhaps smelled) the whale corpse about two miles seaward of the Elbow, and the tiger sharks were still tearing off chunks of meat and blubber. After shooting a few topside photos of the scene, my dive buddy and I decided to view the scene from below.

While I took pictures of the tiger sharks, he covered me from behind armed with the dubious protection of a boat hook. The sharks were obviously well fed by the time we arrived to dive, and we correctly assumed they would not be interested in munching us. But it is still somewhat unnerving to float in 400 feet of water (with no reef visible), in a slick of whale blood, without a shark cage, while a pair of 12 foot sharks swim close to inspect these diminutive interlopers to their free lunch. It was a special marine encounter and we felt privileged. Most divers never get to see the spectacular marine life that passes the Keys borne by the Gulf Stream, but from sharks to dolphins to turtles to whales, it is all there.

Also resting in the deeper waters offshore

are the twin 327 foot U.S. Coast Guard cutters **BIBB** and **DUANE**, intentionally sunk as artificial reefs the day after Thanksgiving in 1987. In the time they have been on the bottom, the BIBB and DUANE have attracted marine life and divers in almost equal numbers.

The acquisition of these venerable military craft was a collective effort of the local community which took nearly two years and $160,000 to accomplish. The Monroe County Tourist Development Council was a prime contributor, and local dive shops donated thousands of dollars and countless man hours to add this welcome diversity to the Upper Keys dive portfolio. The DUANE is the more popular dive of the two since she sits upright in 120 feet of water, whereas the BIBB settled on her side at 130 feet. With a 40 foot beam on each ship, this means that the BIBB is first encountered at 90 feet while on the DUANE the crow's nest is located in only 50 feet of water.

The DUANE wheelhouse is at 80 feet, and the main decks are at 100 feet allowing most of the ship to be toured in a 20 minute no decompression dive. The BIBB will likely be toured at the 120 foot depth, and advanced dive certifications are advised by local dive operators. Both ships have attracted schools of resident barracuda and jack, and large grouper, parrotfish, and angelfish have begun to seek refuge in the wrecks. The BIBB is attracting colorful incrustation of colonial hydroid and sponge, and has grown to be impressively decorated by vibrant invertebrate filter feeders. Because both ships are so immense, repeated dives are necessary to adequately tour their numerous recesses and holds. Since the ships were sunk in an area consistently washed by the Gulf Stream, visibility can be incredible, as much as 200 feet on occasion, but the current may also be a limiting factor. Once a diver is on the wreck, shelter from the current is found, but on some

The USCGC DUANE attracts abundant marine life, fulfilling its role as an artificial reef.

The twin propellors on the BIBB shipwreck are colorfully encrusted.

days when the Gulf Stream washes through closer to shore, the wrecks may not be safe to dive. Your local Keys dive operator will be best suited to advise regarding daily current conditions.

At present officials of the National Marine Sanctuary Program are investigating expanding the boundaries of the Key Largo National Marine Sanctuary perhaps as far south as Alligator Reef or possibly the entire Florida Keys. If this happens (as we hope), the marine life on the BIBB and DUANE, as well as on the reefs to the south, will be protected from spearfishing and other activities that might deplete the marine life.

PICKLES REEF is just two miles south of the Sanctuary and consists of low profile corals in 12 to 22 feet of water. This is an excellent area for macro photographic subjects such as flamingo tongue cowries, flame scallops, nudibranch, scorpionfish, and numerous species of juvenile tropicals. The reef takes its name from what appears to be hardened, encrusted pickle barrels found scattered about near the stakes marking the reef. These are likely small kegs of mortar mix destined for the forts of Key West or perhaps Fort Jefferson in the Dry Tortugas.

CONCH REEF features both a shallow coral concentration and a steep dropoff from 60 to 100 feet. The Pillar Coral Patch is good for both diving and snorkeling and is obviously named for this predominant coral species which is relatively rare elsewhere in the Keys. To dive the dropoff, the commercial dive boats will usually anchor along the edge of the wall with divers gradually drifting past deep water gorgonia, eagle rays, turtles, angelfish, or even an occasional bull shark. Sometimes the current will be such that the Conch Wall is done as a drift dive, but most often it can be dived from a boat at anchor.

The flame scallop is typical of the colorful macro life found along the coral reef.

These mating turtles were encountered on Molasses Reef, oblivious to the dive boats moored all around.

The wreck of the **EAGLE** was funded by local dive and business interests in the Islamorada area, and the success of this project paved the way for future artificial reef projects in the Upper Keys. The ship was intentionally sunk December 19, 1985 in 110 feet of water off Islamorada and remains today one of the Keys' premiere wreck dives. The 287 foot former freighter sits on her starboard side and provides a home for immense schools of tomtate grunt, Spanish sardines, amberjack, parrotfish, and grouper. There are encrusting sponges and hydroids growing on the freighter now, and macro life such as arrowcrab enjoy abundantly fine grazing.

HENS AND CHICKENS is an inshore patch reef less than three miles from shore, marked by a navigation light. The reef cluster of star corals resembles a mother hen surrounded by little chicks, if you use considerable imagination. Soft corals abound and spadefish, grunts, angelfish, and even snook commonly inhabit the coral crevices. As is typical with inshore patch reefs, the visibility here is very weather and tide dependent, and may range from 15 feet to 60 feet or better.

DAVIS REEF has become an interesting shallow dive frequently included on the itinerary of the Tavernier and Islamorada based dive boats. With dense concentrations of sea fans and gorgonia adding color accents to the low profile hard corals, the undersea topography is fascinating, but it is the marine life that makes Davis unique. Here are green morays that have been hand fed by divemasters, nurse sharks lurking under the coral ledges, and immense schools of grunt and goatfish. These reefs, along with other favorites including Alligator Reef, the Matecumbe Dropoff, and several different historical shipwrecks, make the waters off Tavernier and Islamorada perennially popular with Keys divers.

The EAGLE attracts huge schools of tomtate grunt seeking the protection of the shipwreck's holds and crevices.

Alligator Reef is one of the popular dive sites off Islamorada.

Middle Keys

The Middle Keys are geographically situated between the Long Key Bridge to the north and the Seven Mile Bridge to the south, encompassing the major population center at Marathon. Since the earliest days of Marathon's development, coincident with the advent of Flagler's railroad, the sounds of the swinging hammer have been replaced by the deep throated growl of diesel engines, as Marathon has evolved as a sportfishing and diving vacation center.

Today most of the resort activities occurs between Duck Cay and Marathon. Along the highway in Marathon is a conglomerate of gas stations, strip shopping centers, restaurants, bars, and office buildings. Highway construction is now complete and traffic can move quickly through town. Instead, linger a while. Behind the urban facade, just off the main stretch, are quiet residential streets, secluded beaches, golf courses and tennis courts, and resorts and restaurants from the economical to the upscale. Several excellent dive operations are scattered throughout the city, and these shops serve all possible interests of the traveling diver including daily reef excursions, night dives, wreck dives, underwater photography, spear fishing and shell collecting, or even complete career development programs for those wishing to instruct scuba.

Like Carysfort Reef to the north, **SOMBRERO REEF** is marked by a large lighted tower, and consequently yachtsmen unfamiliar with the waters will be drawn to the beacon. Local dive charters frequent the area as well to view the immense spur and groove coral formations and the abundance of marine life dwelling in the sandy surge channels. The depths range from just a few feet beneath the surface to about 30 feet, making Sombrero popular with both divers and snorkelers.

A beautiful coral reef that is also accessible is both blessing and curse. People and boats

A trumpetfish seeks refuge among the colonial hydroids growing along the hull of the THUNDERBOLT shipwreck.

inevitably come to visit. Reef pressure can come from anchors dropped in the corals and divers careless with their buoyancy smashing into the fragile polyps. Only education and ecological concern can alleviate diver contact with coral, but in many places throughout the Keys mooring buoys are being considered as an answer to the cumulative damage that occurs with anchors dropping into the coral or chain and lines chafing across the heads. In the Key Largo and Looe Key National Marine Sanctuaries mooring buoys have already been deployed and boats are required to tie off to the buoys rather than dropping hook. The Reef Relief group has initiated a similar program off Key West, and concerned citizens of Marathon have generated funding for the initial installation of 25 mooring buoys placed at key points along Sombrero Reef.

Marathon offers numerous watersports attractions along both the Gulf of Mexico and Atlantic Ocean.

DELTA SHOALS is another popular destination for Marathon divers. Consisting of a spur and groove coral formation fanning seaward from a sandy shoal, this is a perfect spot for viewing concentrations of elkhorn coral. Photographers wishing to get close to their subjects will appreciate the numerous cleaning stations at both Sombrero and Delta Shoals. Here the need for piscine hygiene may override the natural reticence of the fish, and photographers can work near to their subjects.

COFFIN'S PATCH is not a single reef but rather a collection of six semi-distinct reef structures in 15 to 28 feet of water. Interestingly, a specific type of hard coral seems to prevail at each reef area, although it is probably the pillar coral concentration than is most unusual. Many of the pillar corals have grown quite tall and impressive, but careful inspection will show how they have had to come back from near decimation by uncaring coral collectors, probably in the 1950s.

Farther to the north are the scattered

Right: Pillar corals are especially abundant offshore of the Middle Keys.

remains of the **DUCK KEY WRECK**. At one time a steam powered freighter, the Duck Key Wreck now rests in 25 feet of water, her smokestacks, hull plates, and twin boilers home to schools of grunt and goatfish.

Marathon is home to not only historical shipwrecks, but more modern artificial reefs as well. The **THUNDERBOLT** is a 188 foot ship, once used as a cable layer and then later converted to a research vessel, which was purchased as it lay derelict. The local dive and business community cleaned the THUNDERBOLT so that no ocean pollution would occur when the vessel sank, and also made it safe for diver access. The ship was intentionally scuttled in 115 feet of water just south of Vaca Cut and presently sits perfectly upright with the top of the wheelhouse within 70 feet of the surface.

In the years since the THUNDERBOLT sank on March 3, 1986, the growth along the superstructure has become impressive. A large coating of colonial hydroid has attached to the cable spool, and schools of amberjack are constantly in residence. Barracuda are commonly found in the wheelhouse, and for some reason the grey and French angelfish that reside along the keel seem inordinately large. In addition to the THUNDERBOLT, the swingspan of the old Seven Mile Bridge has been sunk by the Florida Keys Artificial Reef Association as an attraction for both fishing and diving. The area is often swept by tidal currents making it more comfortable if planned as a dive at slack tide, but the abundance of nutrients flowing past have made the structure vibrant and alive with sponge, gorgonia, and other filter feeders.

The THUNDERBOLT was intentionally sunk by the Marathon dive community in 1986, and has become a favorite of visiting divers.

The Lower Keys

The Lower Keys consist of a collection of generally sparsely developed islands bearing the diverse and eclectic names like Big Pine Key, Sugar Loaf Key, Summerland Key, Ramrod Key, Cudjoe Key, and Torch Key. For those who find the Upper Keys too busy or Key West too urbane, the Lower Keys provides a welcome taste of tropical relaxation and excellent watersports. Big Pine Key is the most populous of the islands and best known for its endangered population of diminutive Key deer, but resort hotels and dive operations can be found clustered throughout the Lower Keys. Dive trips may be booked to the coral reefs around **AMERICAN SHOAL**, or to the nearby **LOOE KEY NATIONAL MARINE SANCTUARY.**

Many divers consider the trip to the Lower Keys to dive Looe Key one of the highlights of their Keys vacation. Named after the HMS LOOE which ran aground in this area in 1744, Looe Key Reef is just 5.3 nautical miles square. This lovely reef was declared a national marine sanctuary in 1981, and as such, certain prohibitions are in place to enhance enjoyment of the reef and to preserve it for future generations. As in the Key Largo National Marine Sanctuary, it is illegal to spear fish or collect coral and shells. Mooring buoys should always be used when available, and especially because of the small area of protected reef and the popularity of the reef tract, divers should be scrupulously aware of their buoyancy and not touch the delicate corals. Additionally, hand feeding of the fish is discouraged at Looe Key, and taking lobster is totally prohibited regardless of season. The management of the Sanctuary rightly assumes that too many divers touch or damage coral in their quest for lobsters, so they have banned lobstering in the core areas of the reef.

Aside from the obvious beauty of the Looe Key reef tract, it is unique in that within a small

Mooring buoys at the Looe Key National Marine Sanctuary help prevent damage to the reef from carelessly dropped anchors and chains.

The endangered Key deer are found no where else but the Lower Florida Keys.

area is contained a virtually complete reef ecosystem. The Fore Reef area features spur and groove coral formations as are likely to be found throughout the Keys. Here high profile corals are separated by deep, sandy, surge channels running to seaward. In the shallows of this area is a Rubble Ridge comprised of fossilized coral fragments, broken and crumbled by centuries of wave activity.

The shallow areas of the Sanctuary are basically seagrass meadows. Juvenile and invertebrate life is richly apparent for those willing to give the time for close inspection, but an occasional shark, turtle, or eagle ray will also dart beneath the startled gaze of snorkelers in this area. For scuba divers, the Intermediate Reef and Deep Reef are probably the most popular. The dropoff is fairly steep, and the density of coral and marine life make this area good for both general observation and underwater photography. Sanctuary management are justifiably proud of a unique resource, and are doing their best to preserve a valuable Keys marine heritage.

The Florida spiny lobster is protected in the Looe Key National Marine Sanctuary, and flourishes as a result.

Key West

In terms of resort accommodations, fine dining, shopping, and conch history (conch being pronounced "konk" and signifying something or someone native to the Keys), Key West is the most sophisticated of the Florida Keys. Civilization in the Keys basically started here with Indians and then pirates. First known as "Cayo Hueso" or Islet of Bones, Key West was theoretically the site of a fierce confrontation between the Seminoles and the Calusas which left the beaches littered with the bleached remains of the vanquished. Some say it was cattle bones that gave Cayo Hueso its name, but certainly the vision of Indian warfare along what has come to be known as Smathers Beach is more romantic.

The small coral islet just four miles long by one mile wide was granted to Juan Salas in 1815 by the Spanish government and sold to John Simonton in 1821. Simonton planned the city to take advantage of the deep natural harbor, and plotted streets and development accordingly. Key West rode an economic roller coaster of boom and bust over the years as various industries became prominent.

The wrecking industry made Key West the richest city per capita in the United States during the early 1800's. (Monroe County Public Library)

Salvaging the spoils of shipwrecks once made Key West the richest city per capita in the United States. There were no lighthouses in those early years, and as boat traffic continued to increase, so did shipwrecks. There came to be a competitive business climate in the Key West of the early decades of the 19th century, and by 1822 a federal court was created in Key West just to rule on salvage claims.

Lighthouses ultimately spoiled that profit center, but not before some less ethical wreckers on occasion erected false lights to lure unsuspecting craft on to the treacherous reefs. Jacob Housman was one of the band of Key West wreckers that continually was caught up in conflict with judicial edicts, and finally fled Key West under legal fire, sailing to the uninhabited 11 acre Indian Key and establishing himself as virtual king of the island. Here he prospered, attracting 20 other wreckers and their families, and establishing a three street village complete with post office, personal mansion, and the Key's first resort hotel, the Tropical. All of which of course was brought to ruin when the Seminole Indians attacked in 1840. Housman survived the raid (which he probably instigated by offering to hunt Seminoles for a bounty), but after giving up Indian Key and returning to Key West to work as a mate on a salvage ship, he was crushed to death between two ships just nine months later.

Sponging, cigar making, and salt harvesting from sea water evaporation all at one time or another contributed support to the local economy. By the early 1900s regular boat traffic brought opera, ballet, and theatre to Key West, and when the city was connected to the mainland via the Overseas Railroad in 1912, Key West was established as a true warm weather vacation retreat.

Plans for Key West to emerge as the American Riviera were dashed with the Great Depression. Eighty percent of the island's population went on relief, and by 1935 when the hurricane demolished the railroad, Key West was at the depths of her bleakest "bust" phase. Gradually military presence in the city boosted the economy.

Monroe County had acquired Boca Chica Key, just north of Key West, for a municipal airport, but World War II made Key West strategically significant. The Army took over Boca Chica and built three paved runways, and in April of 1943 the Navy took over, occupying Boca Chica to train pilots for aircraft carriers. By 1945 there were 4,000 sailors in Boca Chica, and their economic presence in Key West helped the city retain solvency. Now tourism is king and boom times have returned.

Key West in 1838 illustrates the development of the city around its deep natural harbor. (Monroe County Public Library)

Key West today is an exciting blend of watersports attractions, excellent resort accommodations, and diverse nightlife.

With excellent restaurants, museums and art galleries, live theater, both tasteful and tacky retail shops, incredible resort hotels, and the Keys' most happening night life, Key West also features the Keys' most colorful resident population. Fantasy Fest is the Halloween celebration that best exemplifies the abandon and eccentricity of the Key Wester, but every night at sunset at Mallory Square shows the prevailing proclivity to party. Here "buskers", street performers walking tightropes, playing bagpipes, juggling, tumbling, and contorting entertain the masses of tourists in the hopes of a generous donation.

Museums (including Mel Fisher's engaging collection of treasure from the wreck of the ATOCHA) educate and fascinate while art galleries present a fine sampling of various media with a tropical theme. Duval Street remains the community's most lively thoroughfare. Duval is listed in RIPLEY'S BELIEVE IT OR NOT as the "Longest Street In The World" because it stretches all the way from the Atlantic Ocean to the Gulf of Mexico, but in reality is only a few miles long. Along Duval are the T-shirt and curio shops, trendy department stores, restaurants and famous bars that are an inevitable beacon to all Key West visitors. Key West is one dive destination where the above water segment of the vacation is easily as rewarding as the time spent underwater.

The Key West dive portfolio begins for most visitors at **SAND KEY**. Marked by an iron lighthouse erected in 1853 but substantially devastated by fire in 1989, the island at Sand Key is devoid of vegetation but is rich with beach. Actually beach is all there is; fine sand, ground coral, and tiny seashells worn smooth by the waves. Spreading seaward from the island are spur and groove coral formations and rocky ledges. Elkhorn and fire coral

The daily sunset celebration at Mallory Square is one of Key West's most popular tourist attractions.

Duval Street features a wide variety of shopping, dining, and entertainment options for visitors to Key West.

prevail, but there are lots of brain corals and star coral heads intermingled.

Sand Key was the first area in Key West to be protected by mooring buoys to avoid anchor damage to the delicate corals as a function of the heavy boating activity the area receives, but now over 60 buoys are in place from the Western Sambos to the Western Dry Rocks. Reef Relief, an organization of concerned divers and conservationists, was primarily responsible for obtaining the funding, coordinating with the local dive community, and placing these much needed buoys.

Sand Key (pictured here prior to the lighthouse fire in November 1989) is a popular destination for both dive boats and snorkel tours departing Key West.

ROCK KEY is just one mile to the east of Sand Key, and offers slightly greater depths with cracks and crevices home to a wide variety of crustacean and fish. The **WESTERN, EASTERN,** and **MIDDLE SAMBOS** are in the same 20 to 25 foot depth range, but will offer a more dense population of tropical fish than will be encountered at the reefs nearer shore with angelfish, moray eels, squirrelfish, bigeye, and a wide variety of butterflyfish in residence. The distance from the Western Sambos to the Middle Sambos is about 2.5 miles, and it is another 1.5 miles from the Middle to the Eastern Sambos, so these must be considered as distinct dive sites. While the Sambos bear superficial similarity, each reef area has unique species predominantly in residence.

Abundant marine life is as accessible to snorkelers as it is to divers on many of the shallow reefs off Key West.

EASTERN and **WESTERN DRY ROCKS**, and **TEN FATHOM LEDGE** will also likely be covered within the weekly Key West dive portfolio. Ten Fathom Ledge features undercut fingers of coral, archways, and shallow caves at the 60 foot depth contour, and is a good spot to view loggerhead and hawksbill turtles, nurse shark, grouper, and as is typical of many Keys dive sites, clouds of yellowtail snapper. Eastern and Western Dry Rocks are further examples of a lovely shallow reef with spur and groove coral formations accented with sea fan and

Right: Clear water, healthy corals, and colorful marine life typify the Keys dive experience.

gorgonia. Squirrelfish, angelfish, lobster, crab, grunt, snapper ... in short the typical Keys marine life portfolio ... is likely to be encountered on these reefs.

Key West also has their share of historical and modern shipwrecks. The **CAYMAN SALVAGER** is the most accessible of the modern wrecks. Originally a 180 foot steel hulled buoy tender, she was sunk as an artificial reef in April of 1985. The ship came to rest on her side, but was righted later by hurricane force wave action. The CAYMAN SALVAGER had her superstructure removed in the shipyard prior to sinking, but the open holds provide refuge for baitfish, grunts, and occasional grouper. Amberjack and snapper commonly swirl about the ship's exterior.

The **ALEXANDER** bears interest as a dive site under the right conditions. Built as a destroyer escort, the ALEXANDER sits upright in just 35 feet of water, but it is on the Gulf side of the island. It has been submerged since 1972, and has attracted ample fish populations and colorful growth, but since visibility is often marginal in Gulf waters, it is a "weather dependent" dive. In the summer there can be as great as 45 foot visibility, and occasionally even in the winter can be calm and clear. The primary appeal is the marine life the wreck has attracted, and schools of Atlantic spadefish, snapper, grunt, and porkfish share the submerged hull with barracuda and an occasional jewfish.

The **CURB** sits at 185 feet with her most shallow portions around 120 feet, so this is a deep dive for advanced certifications. The former tug is almost perfectly intact, but the time passes all too quickly at such a depth. The **WILKES-BARRE** is another very deep, decompression dive sitting upright in depths ranging from 145 to 210 feet. A 610 foot Cleveland Class cruiser, the WILKES-BARRE was armed with

Elkhorn corals and bluestriped grunts are commonly encountered along the Key West coral reefs.

12 six inch guns clustered in four turrets of three each, and 12 five inch guns in six turrets of two guns each. Beyond the depth range of most sport diving enthusiasts, the WILKES-BARRE is available only as a staged decompression dive, and while there is little time permitted at such a depth, the historical perspective of such a massive military vessel coupled with the incredible parade of pelagic marine life make the dive tempting to some.

The day diving potential from a Key West base is good, but if time and weather conspire favorably, a cruise to the Marquesas Keys might be arranged. Representing the only known atoll in the Atlantic Ocean, the Marquesas are probably the remains of an ancient meteor strike. Visibility and fish populations are better, probably because their distance from shore reduces diver pressure and effects of urbanization on the reef. Overnight trips to the Dry Tortugas may also be arranged through your Key West dive operator when weather conditions are favorable for a crossing.

Fort Jefferson in the Dry Tortugas is accessible by seaplane or boat.

Conclusion

Throughout the Florida Keys divers have come to expect and appreciate convenient, quality dive sites served by professional dive operations. With so much of the local economy dependent upon sport diving activities, the visiting diver is made to feel welcome. With the shallow depths common on most reefs, buddy teams are allowed to dive at their own pace without the constraints of organized guided dives, but for those requesting more personalized services, it is available. With easy auto access, superior resorts accommodations, and a complete tourism infrastructure geared towards water sports, the Florida Keys continue to attract both experienced and novice divers in ever greater numbers.

Left: A snorkeler views the shallow coral reefs surrounding the Carysfort Tower off Key Largo.